CW00631815

ROBERT GREGORY

River Time

For Gemma.

Best Wishes

Robert Gregory

All poems written by Robert Gregory in Cambridge, England.

Part I   March 2nd to March 24th 2012
Part II   June 6th to July 25th 2012
Part III   November 1st to November 30th 2012

Copyright © Robert Gregory 2014

Published by Cambridge Editions
Unit 2, Burr Elm Court
Main Street, Caldecote
Cambridge CB23 7NU

The right of Robert Gregory to be identified as the author
of this work has been asserted in accordance with Section 77
of the Copyright, Designs and Patents Act 1988. All rights reserved.
No part of this publication may be reproduced in any form or
by any means without the written permission of the publishers.

ISBN: 978-0-9576358-6-9

Produced by Cambridge Publishing Management Limited.

Printed and bound by CPI Group (UK) Ltd, Croydon, CR0 4YY.

About the Author

Robert Gregory was born in London in 1957. He was schooled in London and Hertfordshire. He graduated from Churchill College, Cambridge, in 1982, where he read History. For more than 25 years, he worked for an engineering manufacturing company. He lives in Cambridge.

What in me is dark
Illumine, what is low raise and support
—John Milton, *Paradise Lost*

www.illuminant.co.uk
info@illuminant.co.uk

Illuminant
Box 224
23 King Street
Cambridge
CB1 1AH

Contents

PART I

The Old Front Door

I know the score
With the old front door,
And that's without a doubt.
I seldom have to worry,
I never have to shout.

Even if I'm out of town,
Or if I'm far away.
It's always there to greet me,
Each and every day.

It gives a reassurance,
It settles doubts and woes.
It seldom takes a liberty,
It always, always knows.

And when it shuts behind me,
Each and every day,
It has the common decency,
To keep the rest at bay.

River Time

If it is God's truth, I am to tell – then I had better get it right,
At the beginning. The chalky start, in plain old Essex lands is
    not for me.
And I have never made the effort to get acquainted there.
    Instead I wait at my
Commencement, for the river to meander all its own, to meet
    me, as it can,
Once the journey is already underway.

With expansive sighs it comes through Grantchester Meadows,
    offering
Salutations, with strong indigenous trees, to mark the passing,
    left and right.
But then it meets the town and down the years, we've squeezed
    it, with a vice
Of buildings, locks and bridges, bank to bank, from either
    side.

Here, it runs compressed, past medieval courtyards; baroque
    Cathedrals of
The mind, the clipped and tended college lawns; and under
    resolute
Stone built bridges, that speak in a calmer tongue, of times
    when traffic only
Came, without the mean machines of bumper latched on
    bumper, we all
Skate through, on our daily grind.

At Magdalene Street, it meets the place where the City gets its
     name.
And in a time before the first steeple house was made, men
     and all their
Beasts of burden, sort to make the journey, either way from
     east to west.
At this spot, the eponymous crossing point took hold and grips
     in resolute
Devotion; a grip never loosened, to this day.

But I'll let it pass by and drop, at Jesus lock; and fall another
     level to the one
That's soon to greet me here. And as I join it now, an
     exhalation of aquatic
Relief spans its course, from bank to bank, sighing, as it
     stretches slowly to
Itself again and is becoming now, what was ere long intended.

Across the way repose the Boat Houses, that speak of team
     work, where
Every sinew strains the oar to cut the waters glide, a fraction
     beyond the
Competition. On my side, the narrow boats, hug the bank with
     a roped
Embrace and pass a ghost of chimney smoke, to fit a needy
     menu.

At the Green Dragon Bridge I can recross to the northern side
     and here
Beyond the Pike and Eel, that was, and is now boarded shut
     awaiting its
Fate, the tow path takes a hold of my journey and leads me on,
     past gardens
Side by side, where the wooden gate of each, provides an exit.

[4]

Here, the noises from afar die off and back to their beginning.
    Here, the call is
Water born; the surge of eights propelled by urging coxes
    burst, with all the
Power that corpuscular, oxygenated, muscles will allow. The
    novice crews
Tend wearily bank-side and watch them pass, with a nervous
    admiration.

Up and down they cruise – all the way to Baits Bite Lock and
    Weir. Past the
Wide embrace of gaping fields: the leery cheer of pub bound
    folk on picnic
Benches, taking in with warm embrace, all of this time of year.

Now it is as if we – or some of us – can with the river's services
    dispense.
And having used it all thus far turn back, the way we came. But
    with another
Drop, it carries on again – but in a calmer vein expands its
    breadth; digs
Deeper in itself and moves along, to a pace that is a melody all
    of its own.

Here on the far bank, willow trees lean out at angles that defy
    the fall,
Only by roots levied deep and strengthened year on year, on
    year.
And if you give a moment to the pause, their sinuous
    overhang, stops just
Short of the river's surface gleam, that in a given velvet light
    reflects, with a
Mirror's truth, all that's caught above.

And as a wide and sweeping bend hoves into view, the dead
    skeletal frame of
Trees, long given over to the claims of ivy creepers and the
    nervy buzz of
Tireless wasps, who tend their wares from dawn to dusk this
    season long,
Stand sentinel-like, to guard the river bank and send the
    passing traveller on his way.

Catching all of this, I drop down on my heels and take the
    moment, held all of
A sudden in one breath; when, head down, charging fit to
    bust, a wispy stoat,
With black tipped tail, bounds the stone chipped tow path and
    on, into the
Reed high grass, that fringes the river's curving bank of clay.

Safe and out of sight from all the ill he imagines, that I would
    never do him,
He is safe to contemplate a spot of brunch, or do as I am
    doing and
Watch the world meander, in lines of water light and on to
    places far away.

Now both of us are left to take upon ourselves, the rasping
    screech of an
Angry moorhen, who cuts the silence down to size and
    splashes loud with
Flaying wings and stomping feet, running upon the water and
    moves away
Upstream, past a metal barge boat, that floats in grim
    reproach, waiting
Desperately, for a purpose yet unseen.

And here, with a dignity of one that's born to rule, a swan of
    such a state,
Sails into view. And having taken in all that's here, he bob tails
    up and gnaws
The river's reedy bed, taking time with his submerged repast
    and all the while
Leaving to view, an iceberg decked in whitest plume, from the
    waterline up to
The peevish, wiggling tip. Before he rights himself and gives
    back to me, a
Gaze of full reproach, behind his swathed and dripping beak.

He pauses just enough to give me further thought but soon
    moves on to
Matters best for him. And in the distance, over the pillbox
    bunker that was
Put there, to save us at the death, the train from Ely, with
    carriages of four,
Breaks the line between the corrugated land and the endless
    sweep of sky.

All of its own it ponders not a jot, for this or any other view
    and carries on to
Beat the clock and make the station, proud. And as it departs
    my line of
Sight, I am caught as one who is lost in the night; for though it
    is still the full
Girth of a bright, translucent day, I realize now, that I am here,
    not at my own behest.

But at the call of something more – I am now on *River Time*.
And as a formless cloud above, begins to shed its soaking load
    and as each
Drop hits the water, it ripples in repose, a target out from that
    spot and fills
The whole, all for a greater good; as it should and as it well
    knows.

Just as each lock causes but a pause in the voyage each drop of
    water takes.
Just as we think we have control from the beginning, so the
    river pauses, only
At our behest but never will desist, from its intended purpose.
    The course for
Which it was made, is all its own. Not ours – and never will be.
    So unlike the
River's run, I must turn back and leave it to join its friend, at
    the turn of Pope's Corner.
There the Cam will end; and with that end, becomes another,
    greater still.

Perhaps, this sinewed mess of flesh and bone, is not so
    un-river-like, after all?

The Rhino Poacher's Lament

I make my living killing rhinos,
I track them at the dawn.
We fill them full of bloody holes.
And buzz-saw off their horn.

They're a large and docile creature
And seldom seem to hide.
But then it must be difficult
Given all their size.

Once they're riddled with bullets
And dying in the mud,
We start a-hacking and a-sawing
And we're often caked in blood.

When we've killed and desecrated
And left the corpse to rot,
We sometimes stop and examine the horn
And see just what we've got.

There isn't a single ailment,
Hitherto known to man,
That this isn't guaranteed, to relieve,
By any kind of plan.

It cures woodworm in the fingers,
And Beatles on the knees.
They're not like Paul or Ringo,
They always make you sneeze.

There was a boy in old Hanoi
Convinced that he's a prince.
We gave him a slice of rhino pie
And we haven't seen him since.

Some poor soul, near Beijing
Was convinced he was about to die.
We fed him a slice of Rhino horn,
Now he thinks he's Zhou Enlai.

Those who say it's nonsense
And you're better off in bed,
Can't see how it stops a walrus,
From dancing on your head.

There's loads of other contagions.
And it settles every one.
Night and day, in any old way,
And it's always bags of fun.

So chin up Mr. Rhino
And look me in the eye.
I'll try to make this painless,
It's time for you to die.

But sometimes the best intentions
Don't always make the grade.
I was convinced that I would do it,
I had my fortune made.

But as I checked the target
And turned my stance to set,
I realized this was something,
I never would forget.

He's the last one left standing
And all the rest are done.
He's a bit like dear old Jose,
He is a *Special One.*

We've wiped out all the others
And now the news came through
That rhino horn is worthless,
It's the tail on a gnu.

That's where all the money's now.
They'll pay you cold hard cash.
I think there's one in Timbuktu,
I think I'd better dash.

I hope I get there soonest,
I hope they're all not dead!
If I find myself missing out this time,
I'll have to shoot myself, instead.

Sunny Hunny Days

Once or – if we are lucky – twice a year, we make the effort;
We raise the cheer. To reconnect with all our selves, in a
    setting new and
Bold, that brings out something different. That lays a richer
    gloss upon the
Ones already there. That unwinds. But also tempers.

Timing is everything; and seldom easy.
But we get there – eventually. With lots of planning, to and fro.
October on the Norfolk coast. Golf and beer and perhaps
    some sun?
Tea and toast. And all the fun – legitimate – that life past fifty,
    still provides.

Four by fours are rugged things – and need to be.
With us no space is left unfilled. Shoulders locked side by side,
    we pack like
Jack, in his box, all ready to spring forth, once the doors are
    opened.

Hunstanton by the sea. I've been there once, I'm sure...I
    think... maybe...
Can't remember when. Past King's Lynn and Sandringham
    Is near, so if all else fails, perhaps... No!... perhaps not.
We'll stick with what we've got.

They are pleased to see us, when we disembark. 'Hello' and
   'Welcome' – all
Of that. 'Nice of you to arrive!' Here's rooms one, three and
   five.
And once we have unloaded and are ready and set, a taxi takes
   us past
Georgian halls of splendour and fields ordered by walls of
   symmetric stone.
Here graze herds of cattle, in need only of nature's bounty
   and a tad of human kindness.
Actually – that's us as well. But we'd better not dwell upon it.

We hit the town and its people now who hove into view. All
   shapes and sizes,
Ones and twos and corpulent groups, seeking relief from the
   week just
Passed. Looking for something that will raise a spirit or give a
   laugh.
And again – that's us. But let's not dwell there either.

We're not your average crowd. Nothing too exalted you
   understand. Just different.
You won't find us on any old shelf.

So we disembark and pick our spot. The vacant picnic bench
   might have our names brass plated on it.
Facing out towards the sun, that fifteen minute wait, made the
   first draught
Taste just great. Now we are truly here. Cheers boys! Here's to
   us!

Between the conversation breaks – as old jokes
And new ideas, that came and went, as monies earned and
Monies spent – the pauses, summon ghosts of empires
    unclaimed;
Now passed by – and out of reach. In this life, at least...

And sharper still, in vivid outline, shimmering red,
The dagger-eyed spectre of plain 'Regret', stood stark, in silent
    accusation. They passed no sentence, save what their
    presence by the moment meant.
But circled us each, in weary approbation – still.

And as the Sun moved lower down the Wash, in search of
    morning in
Another land, the starting gun for Friday Night, rang – loud
    and clear,
As a band, throughout the town.

Now butchers lads and drug store cowboys, join the ranks of
    quirky girls –
Who skipped and wove the narrow pavements, past the
    chipped and boarded
Stores, the fraying charity shops; and the few remaining
    outlets of artisan endeavour.
All in search of salvation.
Of such a sort; as times like these provide.

Here slabs of beer, in cans too warm for good, need chilling
    soon. And lottery
Tickets offer, through a needle's eye, the hope of new
    tomorrows.
And if it all, should pass them by – as it surely will – the
    quench of that chilled
Lager, the apple tang of ice cold cider, will balm the pain of
    days to come.
Until the next time...

The girl in leathers red and black, parading all before us,
Realizes, that we are not for her, on this, or any night.
And fires the engine up and with a roar that speaks of fine
    contempt, departs
Along the front, in search of her own – a younger – kind.

So consolation comes in a brimming cornet full of salty chips,
Too piping hot to barely hold, to scorch the fingers and burn
    the mouth.
A splash of tarty vinegar and a lash of spicy sauce, refuels an
    empty spot.

And as a hazy Celtic drunk, bums a cigarette with slurred
    thanks for our kind
Charity, we pause... and think... and take up one more beer.
Here, to reflect in a land of Camelot and wassail,
The olde ideals of Arthurian England – live on; with just a
    little trimming.

Now as darkness comes, we make our way past the pally dance
    hall of
Yesteryear; the Vegas styled arcade where old pennies, fortunes
    made.
But for now, it all seems just one way.

And in the basement bar, across the road from boarding
    houses,
Steeped in sashed, bay windows of Victorian stone,
Where this evening's diners watch that big old Yankee car, with
    white walled
Tyres, that spoke the glories of Eisenhower's years,
Roll the promenade in endless circuit, one more time.

Here we five – un-conscripted; never bombed, never shot at –
    (save the
Occasional cryptic glance) – over taxed and under valued;
On a weekend summer's run, from past demands and future
    billings.
Here we crack another round and take the cheer from each
    other, as we can.

Here tomorrow's breakfast is all set and the time for the vital
    first swing on the
Tee confirmed. Here the pairs are cut and drawn and a little
    wager laid.
And once the plans are set, we settle back to reflect, on what's
    to come.

As the conversation turns I wonder how the night disperses all
    the day-time
Folk away? And is there really a pillow, ready for every head?
The glasses drained. All said and done, we take the journey
    back.
Last sitting at nine – and we are just in time; avoiding any flak.

Not a whisper of breeze passed that morning, between our
    foreheads and the
Risen sun. And when, past one, we shook hands and left the
    final green, it
Was seen, as a triumph, of a kind. Even if the score was not.

And on the journey back, we relived from time to time the
   shots that nearly
Made the mark. The ones that were 'almost'. As well as those
   that really did.
Like those leaps and bounds at life itself, we came out with
   mixed results.
It is not always what you expect. But if we missed, it wasn't
   Sunny Hunny's fault.

The Graveyard Shift

Every year about November time, duty calls and no mistake.
  Sadly, the pub,
We used to make our rendezvous, the Rose and Crown, is all
  shut down, so
We go directly there, instead. Pity that! For we were famous in
  these parts.

We only came but once each year and every time they hailed
  us like old
Friends, returning from a far and distant land. But it was only
  Cambridge, just
Up the road. And I was sure they were told – and understood.

We gained this reputation, you see. We could not be mistaken
  – otherwise.
They called us 'the Graveyard Shift'; and after a slug of grog to
  fend away
The cold, we made our way, with torch in hand, up the
  darkened road.

At the iron gate we closed it, ever so gentle like – so as not to
  wake the dead.
And with a true respect, born not of ritual, simple or opaque.
  But of
Something, a grant of real understanding, that brooks not fear
  nor dread; but
The grasp of a lean, unalloyed truth.
That we'll all pass this way, one day – for ill or good.

By the silhouette of that ancient church, we gathered round
      the grave and
Stood and passed the aqua vitae to toast the living and the
      dead. To call
Out times when five, once were six. And recall the many days
      when he, made
All the difference between 'remember' and 'forget'.
And those times were more abundant than the headstones we
      could stand to count on that, or any night.

Not by the gleam of armies, monarchs of men, nor those self-
      raised
Messiahs; but in ten thousand places of such respite,
As these, throughout the land,
Are the history of these islands, set out for all to understand.
The reams of figures, stated 'facts' and speeches heard, are as but
Supporting players, to each and every character in their day.
They as one, made the whole, on which we stand.

The small untended plots of raw neglect, creeper strewn and
      grass covered,
A coating knee high – smothered, a camouflage to overlay the
      passing years,
Where beneath, the earth, reclaims itself.
Dereliction, is a story all its own.
But even here there lies – untold – a cause that will, one day,
      find a voice.

And if I raise the torch beam, churchwards, towards those
      ancient
Headstones, where the wear of all the elements, have by the
      seasons,
Rubbed away the markings, once clear as day. Still there can
      be glanced the
Briefest clue of who, *they* were.
'Mary wife of –' and the rest is lost to sight.

And you are left to ponder, on the line of Mary's life.
Above us stars, as old as the ground on which we stand, stare
    back at us,
Each with a tiny beam of light, that is so ancient as to give little
    clue, of where
They are tonight.

In truth, we are all marooned in a time we think is now. At a
    place we are
Convinced is here. And some, for fear, think nothing more
    than that. But
Times such as these set to mind, the thoughts of how, we will
    become all of
This – one day.

As we pass the whisky around and distil that smoked and peaty,
    tang,
That warms our chattering mouths – and crunch the frost, as it
    rises beneath
Our numbing feet. The thoughts of warmer climes and
    something tasty on a
Plate, cross our minds. And with one final bitten swig, we put
    the empty bottle
By the headstone and say a last – 'au revoir old mate'.

We'll carry on tonight inside and pick up all the stories that
    we've missed. And
Try not to kiss away, as many days as we have done before;
    desist.
And try to do a little better – spread a bit of cheer.
We are off now.
'You're always missed!'
We're the Graveyard Shift!
And we'll be back again, next year.

The Smoking Ban

All in a rush and running short of time, a friend of mine and I
    had the chance
To make a brief exchange. To catch up on squandered years
    and the
Occasional missing month, of false fears and half forgotten
    cheers of days up
Mountain tops and half down in the dumps.

The last time we'd shaken hands in long forgotten climes
    before 1999, clicked
Up a second millennium. We'd changed of course – and quite
    a lot – but I had half
Forgot, how much he still enjoys a cigarette.

In years before we would have carried on discreetly as easy as
    drawing
Breath. And he, without a moment's thought, would have
    pulled out some half
Crushed soft pack, flicked the lighter in a flash and with a
    careful draw and
Ten seconds later a well aimed release, exhale; and carry on
    the brief.

No more! For out of doors is all that we're allowed to find.
    And so we stand
Like strays in hand on the cold and skiddy pavements, wet
    beneath our feet.
And in the lights of passing cars, the finer sleets of rain can be
    picked out
Again and again; as the chill of bitter wind stings a nerve
    around my teeth.

And when he had finished like a bolted meal with all taste and
     repast
Sacrificed to quick consumption, we turn to find the latch has
     dropped behind
Our backs; and call and pummel on the door, at last to reclaim
     our rightful sitting.

In football grounds where I used to stand as a boy, there kiosks
     offered only
Cigarettes. Now the smokes, like stanchions, have all gone.
     Dispersed on the
Dispatch box, of a Minister's idea of 'greater good'. And of
     course 'it should be
This way' – they all say – and raise a cheer; 'they' being those
     well versed in
Shouting loudest, as they would.

Another soul, fretful of what she might find, departs beyond
     the door outside,
For a few staid moments of relief.
Whatever's said – against or for –
There is always a smoky warmth within the law.

The Way We Live Now

There are corpses in the river
And helicopters in the sky,
Sirens wailing nightly,
Deafening you and I.

Is this the south side of Chicago?
Where the bullets are dumb dumb?
No. It's a modern academic city,
Built for zest and fun.

There's glass across the pavements
And blood across the street,
Cans and plastic litter
Are scattered at your feet.

If you want to stay connected,
If you want to keep alive,
Don't be disrespected,
In any kind of dive.

Otherwise keep your counsel
And go boldly on your way.
You'll live better in tomorrow,
If you keep safe today.

Other People's Children

When I am feeling charitable – and possessed of rather more
    of it than I am
Right now – I can see how others view their children as
    something more than
A trophy to wave in your face – at any given moment.

That sense of expectation for all the coming tomorrows. The
    idea, that here is
Something of me, that will carry on beyond – must seem real.
    At least for a
Time. So planned or otherwise, the production line, trundles
    on. It's only
Through many bends and far down the road, that ideals long
    held, can be
Seen to have taken flight, or crashed and burned, along the
    beaten track.

In the time when feelings fresh, as to cut raw nerves; and
    elations which gush
Like fountains of the mind, are still held in the palm of
    expectation. And only
When they have spent and gone, or dispersed, to the
    imagination, does the
Blind tramlined ally, of weariness and indifference, take a
    lasting hold.
Until then, there is still – all to play for.

It is not so much the quality – just the numbers that cause me
  that unending
Feel of angst. The sense that another is more than just one
  more than what
We do not already need. And in these televised times, where
  politicians, set
To please with heartfelt squeeze of all that they can reach,
  hoist high their
Squalling brats, like the ensigns on battlefields that seethe
  contempt, towards
The people who sent them hence, the enemies of their callow
  grasp and
Insipid sense of disregard. For them, a feckless sentimental
  gesture always
Holds sway, over the hardened reach of a necessity, that has to
  wait upon another day.

So there isn't much I've missed; or kissed goodbye to. This is
  something that
I am happy to let go and you and all the rest, can decide upon
  it as you will.
The handles on this Cup – are not mine to grasp.

My Friend Sam

Whenever I am through the door,
Whichever way, I know the score –
That he will be, amongst the first to greet me.

Inscrutable with that look,
A stare that says he will brook
No fools at this – or any other minute.

At the bar, I place my order
And think about, as I ought to –
A seat where I can sit, in full repose.

He wanders off with unfazed ire,
To try his luck beside the fire.
It's a journey, that he full well knows.

At the alcove, by the light,
I adjust my focus and raise my sight,
In full contemplation of the world today.

There's little good and too much bad.
It's something that is always sad.
But then it always seems to be this way.

Looking down and I can see,
That woolly face staring back at me.
He thinks these next few minutes, I'm for him.

With a single bound he's on the seat,
He settles down, it's really neat,
The way he's decided, today I'm not so boring.

Fifteen minutes have passed us by,
Then I start to ask him why,
Such and such event's turned out this way.

Disarming, calm and un-shook,
He gives me an abiding look
'You're bonkers like the rest' he seems to say.

With due regard for his point of view,
I think we'd have to say, it's true.
We all come up a little short in his respect.

We think it's us, he fits in with.
But in the line of take and give,
I think we'd suffer most from his neglect.

With one bound, he's on his paws
And off in search of another cause.
To check out the new bods, just come in.

He causes me to think and blink
And order up another drink.
Did I really say that I was smarter than him?

Head Out On That Highway

Billy cried in hubris, I'm sure you understand.
Wyatt said 'we blew it' – on the other hand.

Between the two extremes; the sifting of fear and dread.
The pain of never knowing, if you're alive or dead.

The hope and expectation that takes you round and round.
That spins beyond indifference, towards another town.

The sense of keeping moving, the fear of hitting – 'Stop'
For some it's always showing. For some it's all they've got.

So let's just keep on going, turning on the road.
The rainbow's ending shortly. Who knows where it goes?

This is a hallucination, a clinging sense of dread.
See me in the graveyard, when we're home and hosed and fed.

I think there's something more to this, a greater part you see.
The better part of what I have, is the part of you, in me.

Writing

Writing is a curious take
A very selective way to make – a living.

For only some it can be done
And for fewer still, is it really fun – or willing.

It's singular; devoid of overhead.
A pen, a desk and perhaps a bed – not a lot for just a shilling.

Now we have moved on a stride.
Out of doors or inside – todays demands, demand you type.

To get the best of all that's said
You have to mine inside your head – and do your best to get it
    right.

Think about it! Set it down!
Don't let your ideas be pushed around! – One day they will see
    the light.

Until that day comes, it's hard to say.
When will be the judgement day?
Conviction's all. I think you'll find.
Stay the course and hold your mind – that's the friend to see
    you win the fight.

Marking His Passing In The Local Rag

We're so sad, you just dropped dead,
We really miss you Uncle Fred.
We hope you find yourself in clover.
We're really sad and so is Rover.

We think of all those days of cheer.
Especially those when you weren't there.
It's our greatest hope and all our wishing
That it's Marilyn Monroe that you're kissing.

When you've finished and through with that,
You'll be back together with Auntie Pat.
We'd like to wish you lots of joy.
From life's shore we shout 'Ahoy!'

Heaven was made for you, you know,
There's nowhere else for you to go.
Well nowhere else that we can think.
So we're off now to have a drink.

Goodbye Uncle, you were the best.
It's time for you to have a rest.
There was never another, that we would choose.
We hope you enjoy your heavenly snooze.

David the Dog's Modernisation Project

David the dog was bred superior;
You could tell it was true from his gleaming exterior.
All of his friends were just the same.
Even his breeding was a coveted name.

Worried he might be left on the shelf –
One day determined to better himself
And not just himself but all of his kind –
He called an assembly of those with like mind.

'We need to transform and we need to be seen
To arrive at a point where we've never been.
So it's up off four legs and straight onto two.
That's the way forward, for me and for you.'

'Are you sure about this?' came the doubtful reply.
'Of course I'm sure!' he said with a sigh.
'And furthermore – we're friends; it's the way we behave.
And by the way – please call me Dave'.

But some sour skeptics were far from convinced
And lifted their heads from their biscuits and mince.
'So what is our purpose on this earth right now?
What are we for? And how should we know?'

But Dave was determined for them to say Yes.
He knew what was worthy. He knew what was best.
'If we get it right, the rewards will go far.
There'll be no more 'Walkies'; we'll be driving a car.'

'And that isn't all. It isn't just walking.
We're going to devise a new way of talking'.
A wise old St. Bernard said 'A new way of talking – How?'
'It's simple' – said Dave. 'Just listen to me – *Meeeoooowwww*!'

Salutations to Our German Friends

The time is here and long since come,
When we should be as one, in acknowledging those,
Once so long our foes and now ere long our friends.
That curious national psyche that holds times; old can
Still call the shots in the here and now – seems sour, at best.

The infantile insult that proclaims, history in the lands
Beyond the Rhine began, in all we see, in nineteen thirty-
    three.
And came full stop, in nineteen forty-five. It is not a myth to
    keep alive.
Not with Schiller, Goethe, Charlemagne, or even if you will
    Attila;
Though he was, actually, not German, in any modern way.

And although we sometimes say, we need to keep the Krauts at
    bay –
The country is awash with all their products. Precision
    engineered cars,
Electric razors, mirrors, fridges, gadgets and machines, all
    gleam on the
Roads and in the houses of this land, at any time of day. And
    as for the
National obsession of football – let's just say, we should be
    grateful, that
Cricket has not yet caught on in Berlin.

So the deluded and vindictive little man, with his purloined
     Hindi sign,
Should be left in his own time. A part of history he may be but
     he's not the
Only one to see. And if we could raise our game the same and
     think of
Adenauer and others as well, it would best for all, truth to tell.
     A future
Is never made, by just selective glances and aspersions, looking
     back.

It's not another confidence trick we need but something to
     plant the seed, of a
Beginning far from new, because we're each ancient as we
     stand but
Proffering an open hand – we can spin the march of time,
     forward, at a rhyme,
That makes the needs of both, capable of achievement.

But there is just one more thing to recall before we turn the
     page.
Not in any given age, has a country done what the Germans
     do.
With stone cold, unflinching eyes, they look back at all whence
     they
Came, not as some Teutonic Uriah Heep but with the courage
     not to shirk a
Sight, that's sometimes awful. The Gorgons of their past,
     require no
Reflections on a shield, in their hands.

It's our present that always causes us to flinch and look away.
    Often back to a
Halcyon day, that can have more than a touch of imagination
    about it. If our
Leaders could find the time to spend less of it on their knees,
    pleading for a
Cause that was never ours to begin with – Please? That could
    be our new
Beginning – of a sort – as well.

Reckoning

Nemesis follows hubris
Every single time.

Nemesis follows hubris
Right the way down the line.

Nemesis follows hubris
If you think it isn't so.

Nemesis follows hubris
It'll tell you where to go.

Nemesis follows hubris
Just when you think it's not.

Nemesis follows hubris
And takes away the lot.

Nemesis follows hubris
Without a starting gun.

Nemesis follows hubris
Catching everyone.

Nemesis follows hubris
It's quicker than you think.

Nemesis follows hubris
Before you've raised your glass to drink.

Nemesis follows hubris
Like the tides across the sea.

And if I catch the latter
The former catches me.

The Supper at Emmaus

There are occasions when I find, that I have the luxury
Of time on my hands for just a day. And if I can find the way
To cast aside pauses and excuses old, parcelled as something
Fresh and cut the step, to make the train, at the gate. I can
Take myself, London bound.

Not for the shops or the joy of being still able to weave, as I did
    in my
Halcyon days before, when I still had hair and a figure trim to
    match,
That let me race with a twist in every game, to win the day and
    make the
Score. But now through crowds of office folk, shop workers,
    the guy,
The girl, the bloke who's always there. Or perhaps just
    someone marking time.

And in Trafalgar Square, you can pause at St. Martin's gates,
    and reflect not
On the dosshouse student types, with backpacks bulging fit to
    burst,
Sprawled across the steps, like fallen soldiers; bowed but –
    thankfully for
Them – unbloodied. You can think of Nell – the feisty squeeze
    and please, of
Charlie Stuart. One of all the many, he picked up and
    discarded, day and night.

Or if something more of us, is closer to the mark and you
    need to raise a
Laugh – at all times – and none more so, than we do today.
    Then we can
Think of Mr. Hill, to whom Anthony Burgess, no less, said the
    last farewell,
Within these very confines. Benny was just like Nell; both knew
    full well the
Way their world unfolded.

Beyond the crowd's piazza-swirled embrace, where Nelson's
    face and
Washington's regal pose hold the day, a quieter throng awaits
    in the gallery
Beyond. And if I am in luck, I can find space, as well as peace
    of mind, within
The awe, of all its vaulted settings.

How a man of cards, dice and blades, always ready for the
    fight, gave rise to
This and such others, is at first sight hard to fathom. Perhaps
    that ferocious
Pulse, that ceased, on a Tuscan beach, at Porto Ercole, could
    not distil the
World in any other way. He was, as he was – because; and not
    despite. And
Like his subjects, he reaches out to us in chiaroscuro light.

Ostensibly, it is one still life surrounded by four men. But the
    mastery of the
Moment creates the deception of a camera's eye. The shades
    of all and the
Shadows, cast behind, find a depth that makes us reach, not in
    benediction
But to that fruit basket, in the fore just beyond our latent
    grasp, about to fall.

Christ, in rejuvenation, risen fresh from death, draws into
    himself all of the
Moment. Cleopas gestures wide, incredulous in recognition
    and his fingers
Seem enough, to be a part of us and not the subject. The
    other, no less in
Awe, makes to ascend, astonished, at the greater elevation of
    another. Now
They are disciples, unencumbered by the sluggish foot of
    doubt. Just the
Innkeeper appears as one of us, a spectator captured by the
    moment.

The pilgrim's shell, the chicken for the feast, the cap upon the
    head, the
Weave of all the cloth and the sturdy cut and plane of the
    chair back, are all
Parts, that fuse each to the greater whole. The shadows upon
    the wall, recall
A dance of shades before the night.

And if your mind allows, you can feel yourself, stepping
    forward, unseen, into
The canvas, holding all to view and allow your eyes to follow
    the scene
Through, to the conclusion, as you hold it. Now canvas, brush
    and oils desist,
As you move yourself, into a past so near; but also ages,
    smothered ages,
Before our time.

Few can pick the subject, less still capture a scene, that asks so
     much of all
Who wish to see it. To pause on our faltering redemption and
     as a quarry,
Renew the pace and make us worthy of all our steps, until the
     last. There's
The task – for each of us, on this or any day. Perhaps, seeking
     pardon in
Rome, Caravaggio missed; but found at his last shore, salvation
     with the
Tides, whatever others, then or now, may say.

Doggerel

'Pussy Riot', you understand,
Is a fabulous name for an all girl band.
It's certainly true. It can't be contested.
I'm so sorry to hear, they've just been arrested.

Even the Great McGonagall would say
As he sat by the banks of the shiny, briny Tay.
I was incredulous to read elsewhere, you know,
Of a ladies' fashion problem, called camel toe.

If there's a solution it's possibly found
In putting them together and swapping them around.
Pussy Toe and Camel Riot.
I am sure McGonagall would try it.

The Milk of Human Kindness

Catching the following wind,
Of some gut bound hag,
And her malevolent clan,
All benign intentions they can withstand,
On their way, towards the Grafton one day.
I couldn't help but note.

At a cyclist, one aimed a passing kick,
Another, intoxicated, was violently sick,
Another still, hood up, head down, eyes unseeing
Spun and spat a goblet of ire, untenable desire and
Half realized invective of fire – straight at her.

And she didn't blink, or take in all, or any of this.
And waddled on her way, giving it a miss.
With a manner that spoke, of someone else's problem.
Which, of course – it is.

And I wondered how much for each occasion
She will cost the great British nation?
And I thought of an alternative – like
Sterilization.
Then I thought of the wailing – and all that lament.

So if you're talking monies well spent.
Try a well aimed bullet, with a well aimed intent.
That's not very kind.
So it is as best, you can't read my mind.

God made Man in his own image. Don't forget!
Just as well that. Otherwise, one day, I might really start to fret.

'Big Up' the Factory Men

Even now, looking back at our ascent and fall,
The all of it, seems a tough nut for any table.

I can remember well those days when we simply
Could not get the products out the door, fast enough.

Those times when demand was always several steps
Beyond supply. And supply was always, always willing, the more
    to try.

I never thought we'd hit the end. And when we did there was
    nothing left that even we could do to mend.

I still think of all those weeks and years of great success and
    cheers.
Of orders in and shipments out. But still some time to lark
    about.

Winter mornings freezing cold, the heaters working overload,
By lunchtime the machines had warmed us through.

The heat, the haze of summer days. The smell of oil or sting of
    swarf.
But we seldom flinched and always, always stayed the course.

As demand dried up and fell away. we tried everything in any
    way,
To turn around a losing situation.

I left a part of me behind, the day I walked out the door, that
    final time.

And I tried to look you in the eyes and and tell you how much
I apologize.
But it was inadequate then; and doesn't sound much better
later on.

We've all moved ahead and passed the brow, of that particular
hill.

So, 'Big Up' the factory men! You were something special
then!
And truth to tell – you're something special still.

The Woods

Days, short or long in centuries, way back when, would see
Those who came before us, spend their days bound by forests.
Then, the trees gave shelter, food and reassurance in a world
That threatened so much, to cut and bludgeon, in a very
   different way.

Today, the woods are driven past or sometimes through; but
   seldom
Engaged as places to reside or contemplate the days as wide, as
   they once
Were. We need our trees today – as much – and sometimes
   more, than those
Hardy folk, of the unstraightened past, whose world we think
   of, as but a story.

Glory, for our times, is something well beyond tranquil
   contemplation.
So if I get a chance, to catch the moment and skip across a low
   stone wall,
All ice cold, even in the warmer climes of spring, I'll take some
   minutes to let
A world of bursting floaty leaves and angled branches, hold
   me in a silence,
All of its own calling.

Falling through the bowers, shafts of light rain down, as spears
   upon the
Forest floor, catching extended visions, of insects driven,
   through the risen
Mists, within their core. A butterfly may flutter by and
   through, towards an elfin
Rabbit, the little Norman soul, who long ago, made these
   places home.

[45]

Owning up, a pheasant calls his mark to another of his kind
    and if I stand
Stark still, I can almost think to make the claim, to be the first
    upon this very
Scene. A conceit that doesn't take a droplet of the truth, more
    than an oak
Leaf holds a cachet of newly fallen rain.

Again and again, these trees watch the seasons and all they
    bring, come
Singing in on time and hold the line, as each departs, at the
    calling of
Another. There were woods once, across the downlands and
    though they
Won't return, the remainder of their kind, give us a root into
    the past, whose
Hold we loosen at our peril.

We are not creatures of the wood; but we are from it all the
    same.

I Bow To Thee My Country

We're becoming more corrupt with every passing day.
We've fallen out the first world – and the second's on it's way

As bureaucratic fingers, tighten round your throat,
The art of keeping breathing, is all that's keeping you afloat.

Failure has a currency, all its very own.
Cynicism is it's name; and it never needs a loan.

I've got a regulation. It says that A means B.
It wants you crawling on the land and waltzing on the sea.

Dawdle in the darkness and you might just get away.
Step forth in the morning and you'll find there's hell to pay.

Can you afford to bother and trust it all to luck?
Can you push on to another, with the risk of getting stuck?

You can blame the politicians. You can say they've let us down.
But they're as lost as the rest of us. They're kings, with half a
        crown.

The people seldom trust them – and don't know what to do.
They don't trust the people – and both can see it's so.

We're like Wile E. Coyote, running on the mountain top.
When the land disappears from under our feet, we
        contemplate the drop.

The noise of people falling, is a siren screaming sound.
We're counting down the days left, before we hit the ground.

You feel something has to give. You can't have any doubt.
But you keep on hope on hoping, that it might see your time
out.

You're caught between the extremes, of an overflowing cup.
And being like Mr. Micawber – hoping something will turn up.

I know that some are bailing out and some have already gone.
But I can't retreat again and face defeat. Well, not another
one.

So cross your fingers and brace yourself, for what is sure to be.
This is a battle not quite lost; but it's hard to see a victory.

Drifters

Catching up, the other day, with one of those old-style 1950s
    westerns,
Where the man wanders in from nowhere and, with a spray of
    well-aimed
Shots and an attitude that speaks defiance to any odds, carries
    off the day.
And then moves on, to another call, beyond the wide horizon.
It made me, all of a moment, think of us.

And I got to wondering how it is that we are all just 'drifters'
    now, as well.
Not in movement – planned or otherwise – from one town, or
    venue, to the next;
But how we drift, to and through and from each other, day on
    night on day.
As any other, other than what we have, is what we want or
    need.

Perhaps because we fix ourselves in some town, here or there.
The area then binds us with it's own roots, rather than any
    that we might choose to put down.
We sense the angst of all that may lie, unknown and out of
    sight,
Beyond the bend, just down the road, in any evening's light.
Clinging to what is known and held, we see the sense of the
    dissolute in the faces of our daily lives.

It takes the constant action of many thawing chips, which
    strike with quiet resolution,
To keep the ice unbroken. For time will always set to freeze,
Where and when it can. No malevolence, you understand, it's
    just it's way.
And sometimes it is just a minute or two, less an hour or a day,
Which gives a chill to an occasion where the balm of warmth
    once held sway.

So getting a defiant line, and one that says 'I won't be broken,
    yet!'
Upon the ire of unfulfillment, is a calling, of it's own, that's
    hard to make.
But if we are to avoid the mistake of treating each like the
    ghosts of contemplation,
To be walked through at the command of any given instant,
Then we need a benchmark that we cannot neglect. Try
    looking in the mirror.

And keep to mind, in whatever way you choose to stand, the
    here and now,
Or even if you make the break, to take that bend in all
    defiance still,
A conclusion waits on it's own time and place to make a first
    and final greeting.
Moments squandered now are not for reclamation later on.
When a dreadful darkness closes in unseen, try to meet it with
    the least burden of 'what might have been'.

Do Carry On

'No, no, no! Barbara dear!'
Cried Kenneth Williams, loud and clear.
'Tent up now. Bunk up later!'
I'm sure there were films, probably greater.
But none so readily hit the mark
Capturing the British, having a lark.

That wheezing sense of desperation
Crossed the lines of generations.
Policemen, soldiers, nurses, tourists.
Doctors, cabbies, campers, matrons – purists
of the British way, of facing each other every day.

Gormless Bernie, not quite sure.
Cackling Syd who knew the score.
Or thought as much. To avoid the strife –
Don't let on, or tell the wife.
Especially not if it's Joanie or Hat.
We wouldn't ever think of that.

Then there's Charles Hawtrey – what to say?
Hilarity, combined with blank dismay.
Ever willing, devoid of guile;
He never ceased to raise a smile.
Robbed of more than he could ask.
Mugged for six in the Khyber Pass.

Actually it was filmed in Wales
So comparison with epics, ostensibly fails.
But this neglects the crucial fact
Grandeur requires more than tact.
It should leave something, you can't forget.
Something you're always glad you've met.

When looked at, on that scale,
It's clear the team did not fail.
Often damned, then and now,
The criticism seems a trifle sour.
They did what they did, with a sense of fun
And kept on going – Carrying On.

PART II

You

I was on my third glass, thirty stories high,
Looking down on London's lines, staring at the sky.
This is where I come to, to contemplate the rest.
To get some understanding and think about what's best.

To take the news, digested, and filter through my mind,
All the wrongs, un-righted – in good, or troubled times.
All the baking buildings, basted in a summer's haze.
All the lights a-firing, in a chilling winter's glade.

Now the clocks were moving and the hours were jumping
        forward.
Now the word was given. Spring was a rising chord.
A music for redemption. A symphonic sense of return.
Nothing unexpected. And nothing we had earned.

Fifty-five pages, had scarcely checked my eyes
Or caused me contemplation; or stop, to realize.
The condensation on my glass, the taste of salty cashews.
The moisture cleaned my fingers, as I flicked a page to choose.

It was fifty-six that got me. I wiped a palm across my head.
It gave me the unexpected news. It told me you were dead.
We had not seen each other, in nearly thirty years.
But there was no mistaking. The headline held the fears.

So I breathed a little deeper; reclined back in the chair.
Bit my lip a little and tried to show some care
For all the vanquished moments, the decades past have spent.
To try to understand it all; to see what it might have meant.

To grasp an understanding in all the dark recall.
To hope for something better, as we stumble forward.
Your surge was ever upwards, if it wasn't all success.
The pace wasn't always perfect – the trajectory was less –

Than all you really tried for – but sometimes falling short
Can make you grasp, for sure – you've more than you ever
    thought.
That's how it falls about you – and you have to realize why –
We're like a star, ablaze at night. And not just you and I.

It's all the rest around us – whatever they might suppose.
However far they think they've gone – however further goes
The stretch of their ambition; and the hopes, they hope to
    take.
In the end, any distance run, is mighty thirst to slake.

So I sat there still – just – breathing and overtaking you.
You stopped a little while back and I was of the few
Who've left you down the beaten track and sought to carry on
And the point at which I'm vanquished, is a point that's still to
    come.

This is all a pass at chance. A game of cards and dice.
And sometimes the very turn of it, never will suffice.
A thousand calculations; ten thousand points of recall
Will never pass the main gate, if fate takes leave to fall.

And takes out understanding and leaves ambitions in the fire.
And freezes all emotion and cuts off all desire.
And when you're taken from us, beyond our time and space
And leave us contemplating, the cost; the hopes; the waste.

That's scarce made any better, by the fact we're missing you.
But might come more than tolerant, if we felt it to be true
That there's an absent moment, not beyond recall
That is our own salvation – for you – and me – and all.

And each and every one of us – if we did but know.
And sort to make the best of it, before it's time to go.
You've gone and left me beaten, with half a world unsaid.
I've drained the glass completely now – it's swirling round my
    head.

So just before I force myself, out beyond this chair –
Down the silent elevator, that lifts from here to there.
To a ground that's all deceiving, that invites another step.
To a world that defies believing, in all save what we've kept.

That sense of never dying, willingly from within.
It's all we have related now. It's all our kith and kin.
For all the thought and calculation; for hoping for the best.
We sometimes face the coming hours, with no more than a
    guess.

So when all hands are dealt; and the dice, desperately, are
    rolled
And the numbers still found wanting and the story won't
    unfold
To the ending we all long for but are half afraid to tell
So it often goes unmentioned – which is sometimes just as
    well.

When the present's been shipped out – to a future, that's soon
    the past
And the future's expectation is just a memory to last.
As long as you can hold it and try never to let go.
But never let it get a hold of you – so that you never know –

An assumption of direction, of what you think is best.
This world is the only race you've got; your unremitting test.
So if the turn should burn you and if the risk goes sour
Don't feel it's all deserted you. Go straight into this hour.

I think I'll have to leave it now and take my turn to find
All the expectations that fizz from time to time
Across a gaping memory, that sometimes falters to recall,
But is yet to leave a thought so deep, like you, that won't grow
    tall.

The Wedding Planner

Across the iron grey bridge, all stone clad and smoked with
    the dusts
From ages so distant, as to be perceived, only in memories of
    black and
White. Carried onwards by the lightness of a breeze, that
    gently envelops
With a reminder of its presence, beyond the noisy hubbub, the
    roar of
Passing engines, all of whom seem bound the other way.

Onward, where the mile curves beyond a crossing, and ancient
    chestnut
Trees, who've seen it all before, gaze on at the point of bloom,
    on scenes that
Come and go through each day's breaking light and every
    evening's
Shadowed gloom. As the arc of curve retreats before a
    straightened line, the
Unmistakeable sign of a church hoves into view, beyond the
    avenue's end.

There the knots of stoic relatives and trusty friends were
    gathered: all in their
Finest, to complement the hour. Each with an eye on one
    another, each with a
Little regard for their own; all with attention fixed on the
    couple fresh come
Out, as a pair made whole, under their bewildered, expectant,
    curious, half
Believing gaze. They gave a private cheer – to a very public
    beginning.

And here, uninvited but at a distance safe, across the road, I
    stopped and
Watched; and so removed became an extra at their gathering,
    my invitation
Being delivered on the post of chance, at that very moment.
    And they rose to
It, at that hour and gave smiles broad with truth and joy and
    responded
Wave for wave to each before them, leaving no one out of
    sight.

And minutes came and went like seconds spent and even the
    dipping of the
Sun behind a passing cloud, was but an acknowledgement of
    this moment,
The apex of their time. The limousine pulled round and in
    time a slow
Procession they made their way, with thanks and greetings left
    and right
Towards the open doors.

Confetti swirled in wafts and hurtled clusters, up went her
    bouquet, to shrieks
And waving arms and from somewhere and out of sight a
    catch was made
That may, or may not, proclaim a future. For none had come
    to rate the
Chance, to calculate the probability. This was tomorrow's –
    defined by their
Here and now.

And as I crossed the road, they passed behind me and our
    paths that briefly
Met, unwound and dispersed in directions unknown and lost
    forever to the
Other, whichever way we choose to take. And if I paused to
    stop and think for
Just a moment of their journey, then they had other things to
    grip the mind
And cause the eyes to focus. We were lost to the other now and
    actions
Distiled to memories, long before our leave was spent.

Better – perhaps – to jump and fall, than never make the leap
    at all.
Better – perhaps – not to dwell, on a truth that's better not to
    tell.

The Tree

See the tree, swathed in ivy cladding, wrapped around from
  ground to top, by ropes of
Creepered fingers, bottled green and shiny all of leaf and
  stem. Watch the butterfly flutter
In on a July breeze and pause on a droplet of time, and wait
  for the next current, to waft
Him on, to further of nature's station halts.

Dobin, head bobbin' in the muddy paddock further on, eyes
  down, cares for naught,
Ambles on his way. A day, fraught by grass and hay, made
  tolerable by the friendly
Morning greetings, from his owner, apples and carrots,
  crunched with watering chomps to
Salivate the taste. Fruits beyond the boredom, a trot of the
  daily circuit. Just the occasional
Modest jump, to race a pulse and raise a beating heart.

See the tree, beyond the boundary fence – a dead host. But to
  the eye, embalmed by life.
Stunted but resplendent still. And so much more than I – or
  we – ever will. Half a century
Back and more, branches spread across the pathway, leaves
  rose and fell with each
Season's call. Now it's a prop. A grateful resting place for
  others. A marker post, of sorts,
Along the way between one stop and the next. A place for a
  thousand insects, to make a pause.

Crack my coffin lid, five decades on, from its final glimpse of
    light – and what may be found?
A very good pair of cufflinks – I'll be bound. And if they
    smuggled in a bottle or
Two, it may be pure vintage – for the living, if not the dead. My
    polished, oiled boots may
Yet retain the sheen of years gone by — Maybe? Maybe not?
    But I will be fit for just a
Halloween jape. Clad me up in wig and cape. A Yorick but
    Alas! No joke to tell.

Probably best to leave it be. The cufflinks, the boots, belong to
    me. But feel free, to make
Full use of any aqua vitae. On me it would be wasted and far
    too much is wasted still by
Each in his, or her, own wasteful ways.
Spiralling summer days, deep of light and river blue.
True blasts of bitten cold in winter hours, spin us forward
    towards the coffin years.
But don't hold yourself as the tree, enveloped in ivy's fears.
Just try to grab a taste or two of vintage best – afore ye go!

The Moths in Men

All of a summer's evening, when the sweat box day leaves
    behind a ghost of itself,
Well into the the hours past the set of any day's sun. When the
    world is jolted and this little
Bit of maritime lands, seems shaken, closer to the equatorial
    burn, than ever was its want.
Long after today has sunk into the west and tomorrow is the
    Phoenix awaited yet. At an
Hour when every sound, cymbals hit and drums beat, upon
    the ear with tireless
Exasperation still. A walk down any street – up any hill – will
    force the night along.

When the grain of the door has with the heat, just a fraction
    moved and needs an extra
Pull to thwart the stick. I can extend a glistening palm, all in
    the dark, to re-compress the
Switch and throw a light upon the line of my departure. And
    in a gesture, blaze the lights
And lift away the veil, the darkness always holds. No mystery
    now, imagination, fear
Flavoured, is spent. And in the crawling seconds, as the
    compression loosens, the curtain
Rises and with silent applause, the creatures of the night bolt
    forward – their compulsions to indulge.

Ablaze with frenzy, a moth, with bat-like presence, moves, with
    such a turn of speed
Around the hooded bulb, that he is felt and heard but barely
    seen. The light torments him
With each fragmentary glow and beckons him on, a siren of
    burning watts; an illumination
To a self-willed end. Gun propelled, he smacks the canopy
    with a stunning force and falls
At my feet. Neat and all preserved, he lies upon his wings, legs
    spinning on an unseen
Bicycle and slowly the antennae of his eyes reconnects and in
    an instant he wings himself
Upwards. A little Icarus to his doom.

The sound of his obsession – hit on hit – serenades me to the
    door and as my hand
Extends to grasp the handle, the compression ends and
    darkness, embraces the little
Corridor of retreat and silence – perfect stillness, black
    tranquillity – has me at the second of
My departure. Somewhere in the unlit void, released from the
    torments of the light, he can
Groom his wings and take breath, bound as he soon will be,
    upon another flight. Devoid of
Calculation, he does just as he must. His destruction, is all
    within.

So I'll pull the door and take a halting step, past the ranks of
 sedentary cars; down the
Road where screens of entertainment flicker through
 windows, half curtained to the night.
And the only sounds are the passing strides I make in half
 connected, unfelt light.
A drink, a face, a word for some. 'Got enough to make the
 round?' Another week makes
Its presence felt, before the hour is come. Monies earned;
 monies spent; chances came
And chances went. Another segment gone to ground – buried
 in calculations, seldom met.
Thunder rumbles far above. Better hurry. Or you might be
 caught out yet.

Clawed, Lion of The Mara

There was little time in him, for tomorrow.
Little thought of getting there now.
The idea of regret, was not something he met.
He was driven by hunger this hour.

The pain from his back was abating
But the wounds still caused him to cry.
Sometimes he found, he couldn't lie down,
Now the sun burnt low in the sky.

With a faltering stride, he went onwards.
With just the occasional pause.
The ticks and the flies, all circled his eyes,
But a meal was his solitary cause.

He sensed an enemy coming.
He knew they were there – if unseen.
He'd never back down. He would hold his own ground.
Whatever their number might be.

Ahead was a grass-covered banking.
The hyenas, crested it, as three.
Under their gaze, the lion looked aged,
But he was more, than they would ever be.

With a 'yip' they sounded a warning
And quickened the pace of their quest.
Each turned their head, then they hurried and fled.
The odds determined no less.

It was easier now on the game tracks
To follow the routes of the cars
That fled with the night and returned at first light
But left him alone with the stars.

Now the ripening smell of the buffalo herd,
Caused him to fire his hunger again.
There were hundreds at graze, lying under his gaze.
But one, was just too much for him.

One was all he longed for.
It would see him through to the next.
But his solitary power, was inadequate this hour
And wouldn't be adequate again.

He thought of the pride, he fought for.
He thought of the pride, that was his.
Now it was lost, at incalculable cost
And he'd given, all he had to give.

Slowly, he carried onward.
And the herd was soon all out of sight.
He stopped for a drink and to pause, just to think
Of how it may all yet, come right.

A few good meals could heal him.
Something to give him respite.
To allow him to get back, the strength that he so lacked
To revive him – the sinew and fight.

The river ran right past him now
And never stopped to pause.
It clattered alone, over tree trunks and stone
Neither checking, nor changing its course.

With a cat-like crouch, he lowered his head
And extended his tongue to drink.
And the world weary face, at the water's embrace,
Made him pause, in recognition and think.

On the far bank there came a-bounding
A three ton hippo, in flight.
It was onto the slide, with a short drop and glide
And soon he was lost out of sight.

The river was a sound all of its own,
The blood and the pulse of this land.
It gave and it took – and it washed and it shook
And it baptized in mud and in sand.

With thirst quenched strides, he went onwards
But his hunger would know no retreat.
Now at last he was still, at the brow of the hill
And the Mara was all at his feet.

In anguish he cast his head skyward
And shook his mane at the sky.
With all the strength that he bore, he let forth a roar
This land – this land still… is mine.

And I won't let anything take it.
I'll never give up the fight.
I made it, it's mine! For now and all time.
Whatever the day or the night.

Around him was all silence and stillness
And nothing was viewed that could move
The night's unseen breeze, in the acacia trees
In any other time, it might be good.

Then on the far escarpment
Just when all things seemed to be spent
The sound of a bell, on the breeze, brought a smell
The longhorn cattle intent.

On another night in the Masai Bomba
Penned in from the threats of the wild.
This was his chance, to make good the advance
Here was the food he desired.

Men were not of his thinking
But they were warriors just like him.
They needed to be fed and they were just as soon bled
And they killed, to defend and to win.

He circled around in the darkness
Seeking a point to get in.
From beyond in the dark, he could hear a dog bark
And the rattle of cattle within.

The minutes fell away all around him.
Finally he broke through the gorse
But the tables were turned and the ambush, he learned
Left him trapped with no different recourse.

In seconds they had him surrounded
And he strove in the dark for a retreat.
But for this final show, there was nowhere to go
So he braced, for one last defeat.

The men had command of steel.
The tools, to spear flesh and cut bone
The first blow slashed his face and he roared in grimace
But the next did not come alone.

The herdsman threw the spear downward
With the whiplash power of his arm.
It winged through the dark and at the point of its mark
Burst through him, all of its own.

In a second he fell and lay dying.
Air gushed from his lungs and his mouth.
The blood and the muck, ran out like his luck
The hope that he had, all went south.

The waters of life closed over his eyes
And the world that he knew slipped away.
They gathered around and heard his last sound
And they watched him die with dismay.

For they knew just what was coming.
They realized, this was not just, for him alone.
In the long run of time, his death, too, is mine
And all of us, one day to own.

When the first rays of sun meet the Mara
And there's a roll of the living and the dead,
And the quick know it's time, to get running, it's fine,
What's done, is now done – so forget.

When the mists from the dew, first come rising.
And the grass is slick on the ground
And the last calls of night, take wing and take flight
And the dawn is all its own sound.

With the shadows that covered him vanquished
You could catch the last light in his eyes.
It shone from the furnace, within him un-burnished.
It was not just a gift from the skies.

In the moments that came with the new day,
You could still catch the glint of its burn
Very soon now, it will be ended – and how.
Very soon, never to return.

His mighty roar was all of a silence.
His limbs were stiff without power.
In an instant, he ceased and with death was released,
When his life fell away at that hour.

The months and the years have buried him.
And his corpse is now ashes and dust.
But his blood still flows, in the lions like those
Who with caution and doubt, still greet us.

His spirit still straddles the Mara
Like the river that comes from the sky.
The echo of his roar, rides the wind, to the score
'King of all I survey' – that is I.

The Crone Zone

At first, it is a land so far removed from your every daily day
    that its existence
Is but a seldom given thought, far past an unseen horizon, that
    may be out there
But only comes for others – and not for you. And if your early
    days, lack the full
Rhyme of resolution, only found, forged in decades spent, of
    give and take, the sense
That 'this' cannot ever fail or even melt away, is all pervading
    'then'.

But like hot sand, clenched with muscular determination, in a
    glistening fist, of 'What I
Have, I hold', the tighter the squeeze, the weaker grasps the
    whole. And to the unbelieving
Dismay of every combatant, of life's little days, the more you
    try, the less you seem to
Grasp. The further to press the point, the more the time
    seems out of joint, devoid of what
You really will.

Through every mid-day moment and a millennia of midnight
    calls, the fall and rise
Of each passing day, accumulates with imperceptible resolve,
    the seeds of an
Inner decay. The suit that used to fit so neat, now hangs vacant
    in retreat. The tightened
Jaw, so steel sure, is less certain now, in silence or jabbering
    waves of sound. Now devoid
Of other cares, your hair will style itself. And whether willed or
    no, you'll find yourself,
Glaring with a jealous shine, at those coming up the path,
    you've long left, so well known.

The remedies for all of this aren't even simply less, of what it is
    that keeps you going on.
The peps and fuels of life are all its own corrosions too. Like a
    berg, current held, we are
Swept in churning motion, spinning down the ocean years,
    certain of our stride but
Lessening all the while – even if we don't see it yet.
But when you're here – relax! No need to shout. Once in,
    there's only ever one way out.

Alone

Stand, if you can and hold a moment close to you, in
    surrounds sunlit, or closed
By the charm of any night. And pick a place, whose face, is
    seldom seen as the sweep
Of feet, tightly packed and heading all, where all the others
    seem to want to go, close it
Off to no more than a passing sense of acquaintance, that
    might be all the better, if
Circumstance would only let you come to terms, with how in
    tranquil moments,
This is what it really is.

A station halt's the place to start, beyond the midnight hours,
    where the vast terminus
Echoes from canopy to platform, not with waves of people
    fresh come out from carriages,
Dragging half their world along, in tow. Nor to the jolt of
    timed departures all of a hurry,
Late for some and just too quick for those, still yet to come.
    But now, when the few
Become, each, a single one. A whole – alone; not just the pixel
    of a bigger sun.

Then each can take in, a lot of where they really are. And sit
    dispersed, like dots upon a
Page and contemplate, with only half a sense, that they should
    all be somewhere else.
On wooden benches, wrought in iron, beside high arches of
    stone and spans of steel tubes, glass roofs, pristine from
    Edwardian grime and heaps of other ages soot, stand
Resplendent now and proclaim to those who choose to look,
    this is how we really are.
It is what we were all the time, even if through many different
    climbs, you chose not to know.

The terraces have pretty much departed like the burnt and
    mottled layers of each decade's
Coal inspired ways. They live on, in imaginations still not
    stamped blank by time, awaiting
The hour of their return. But in memories the sweep of
    angled stanchions, warm of
Summer days and bitten through by winter winds, soaked by
    downpours from saturated
Urban skies, embalmed by fog and the nervy exhalations of
    tobacco minded folk, stood on
Vacant days, like the frame of leviathans from the seas, picked
    clean by time, on any shingle beach.

Pause at the door and by the streetlight, come to know, in
    early hours, the only movement,
Falling winter snow. Watch it pile up in descent, on cars and
    roofs and walls; on garden
Pathways, pavement, lawns and give a luminous carpet sheen,
    to pot marked roads and
Gravel tracks unseen. And before – well before – the spoiling
    crush of four wheels or the
Sinuous cut of two, snakes away, from one place to another,
    marvel at a transformation
Soon to go. Hold it for the moment as you can – as you know –
    all this, for you, may, or may
Not, come again.

With these and in a thousand other points of repose, recline
    in time to a beat of your
Own making. Take each occasion as its own; savour each
    awakening. Commit it all to
Thoughts, apt for recollection, when ruck and maul calls forth
    yet more hours of push and
Shove and allows no time for passing fancies, of a quieter
    moment's hungry calling. Then,
The value spent on 'Alone' is fully fledged and rounded.
    Reasoned, sensed and sounded.
So well known.

Hesitations

In hesitating, with a throw, uncertain,
I sometimes seem to rope the moment, anyways.
Seeing a friend who sometimes strides with purpose
Down the city's narrow clustered lanes
I should have done the decent thing, this time,
And hailed him and asked away – how he was;
And what his world was serving up, for him.

But I checked and on he went. And I unseen –
Perhaps? Perhaps not? – Kept my peace for the
Councils of another day. When I would wonder then
As I wondered now, what on earth it is, that I could mention?
Another little gear change, slips and is lost
Along the weeks, undulating, uncut path, at cost.

No point to pause for any cause, won or lost, or undecided;
Just carry on, along the way. Our days, so much become the
Vapour trails we see, miles above us in the sky. Some
Trace we leave behind but much of what we do, is lost
To sight. Sometimes cast with slight, well out of mind.
I know; I really should. And it would be better if I could.
But sometimes 'do'– is much easier replaced by 'do not'.

What we have for our digressions beyond our own possessions
Lies in the cast of what it is we are. The star, that we lie under,
Often unencumbered, by any thoughts of what it ought to be.
I could so often have changed this course, if I had the
Time or voice, or a courage, marked by more, than convictions
In the sky. How much better still to keep, the long
Lost missing leap, within the simple sight of my own mind's
eye?

So the ifs and buts, are just as much, the fuel and brakes
For 'Stop' and 'Go' as any medal I might care to show. Not
That I have any close to hand – of course, you understand.
I'll leave that to all those go-getters, who make the difference,
Mark the pages of the news, in papers seen to choose,
And screens that shout a story, marked 'Success'. I'll let them
Pass on by and with just a hesitation, sigh, 'I'm sure it's a way
For them, that's really best'.

Bunhill Fields

Far, far, to the south of here, embossed by age's desert sands,
The pyramids stand, as unmoved by time, as anything a man
Has taken the trouble, ever to set down. But here, on the City
    Road
We do things different – and it shows. In leaves and shadows
    cast,
By beech trees, in a space of open ground, worn down, by the
    living
Of this town, there's an island of the deceased, upon a
    tranquil rise.

In Plantagenet times, this was open ground, beyond the city's
    walls.
The refuse and the dead, lay down head by head, at least it did
    for those
The river had not washed away. And they themselves, were
    packed above
The bones of the Dark Ages, mingled with Saxon folk, devoid
    of
Roman yolk, they left this world in a very un-Roman way.
    Times and lives,
Were shorter, sharper then; and it gave a certain sense, of
    where and
When to go.

And when it came to finding time and place for Dissenters,
    not swallowed up
By the conventions of their day, who cut the bind of Laud and
    Church
And called their Maker, to their lives, very much in their own
    decided way. And
When their window closed, they still sort to choose a place,
    where they might
All of their own design, pass along the way. Friends they were
    then, and
Friends they chose always, so to be.

Here are the women and the men, who made the difference
    then.
The nonconformist heroes of their hour. The progression of
    that steady
Pilgrim, took Bunyan all the way to this. Blake, when he gazed
    on Gabriel's
Eyes, on Peckham Rise, saw salvation closer than he ever,
    otherwise could.
And we still sing – irony withstood – of all his Chariots of Fire
    and the new
Jerusalem of his desire, that he lay down, with all his mighty will.

And on headstones still, the Dissenter's voice proclaims, of
    Southwark
Preachers and Puritan-minded folk, who clung with all their
    fibred being,
To their beliefs and would not fall for others' whiles and ways.
    And they lie
now, with lines of their children, who never made the leap to
    full grown men
But lived and died under their parents' eyes, so often, one, by
    one, by one.
Hard to credit now, the open fields even then, that swept out
    between the

Trees, where shoe box buildings now proclaim, in glass and
    stone, the dusty
Creep of another London borough grown – and in some ways,
    growing still.
Poor Robinson, just like Defoe, marooned by fate's emphatic
    twist, to a misty
World, chock full of silence and regrets. The reflections of
    each passing day,
Layered, like the bones of the bundled dead, when time and
    space, left no
Other room, more. All gone to ground now and closed off,
    since the last little
Girl went this way, on a cold Victorian day, in January, eighteen
    fifty-four.

But in these grounds, lies, wisdom – ages old, as well as coarse
    strivings,
Lost longings, dawns that never came, prayers denied and
    spent, actions
Bled and heaven sent, forged and gone upon an hour, that's
    now dispersed.
For all our lost regrets, it's not the sun that ever sets. It's us, in
    all our spent
disguise. That sees it different, from what it really is, through
    testing times
And sometimes blank, un-minded, oft un-kinded, unseeing,
    un-regarding eyes.

PART III

Leaving Home

When I crossed the bridge at nine, the darkness and the stars
    were mine.
All the shifting waters, cold below, intoned, with a glint that
    almost
Made the call, to jump and see – find out what the depth
    might be? Pausing, that
October's night, above the lines of tethered boats, bank bound
    and soundless
As the river that held them, crystals on a palm of glass, I never
    saw the dew drops
Forming in slow tears, frozen, on the lines of a piece of work,
    resolute beyond
The stroke of any brush; the cast of any hand. And off in haste,
    homeward, I returned.

Came the night and winter took its first returning bite. My feet
    left imprints
On the ground as I hurried back towards the town. But at the
    point of last
Night's stand, there, in perfect frozen symmetry, the spider's
    web, made large by
Highlights of hoar frost, stood as an abandoned tribute to the
    dedication of
Its maker. And through the fog of exhalation and the
    wonderment of 'How?'
I, stood and caught by the morning sky, the home he so
    carefully crafted. The
Splendour of each strand linked, equidistant to the other, in
    widening circles, still.

The precision of his little weave, matches any loom of power,
we might achieve.
There were seven threads, anchored to the whole. One ran, a
full yard long,
From a metal bracket, high above and far beyond my reach.
Along the span
Of steel tubes and angle iron, mixed and fast with concrete
tonnage, something
So slight, as to be almost the weight of light, held fast in the
frozen winter air.
Few spare thoughts went his way, from the folk that trundled
past, into the depths
Of their own day.

So I put my time to another side and cast a thought to the
faith, which caused
Him to abide and put in place a thing so fine, only to see it
rent, from purpose
To display. From function, to brittle frosted art, transformed in
hours of winter's dark
And now in full view, for the eyes of any, who took the time to
stand and look.
Better take it in. The seconds are running down now. And the
temptations for
A passing fist, to cast it all towards oblivion, without a first
thought, nothing missed,
Is as certain as the rising sun. Where's the fun, in thought or
understanding?

So much better to smash and run. Destruction's always so
    much fun. The better
To achieve, the prevention of others achieving. Sometimes put
    in place, the means
Of their not breathing. Stopping there, I tried to fix it in my
    mind and hold its power
In all the morning hours; case them in its wonder. Returning
    back in the misty gloom
Of a darkening afternoon – sure enough, nothing there for
    best. Just a couple of wispy
Strands were left, gummed by moisture to the railing. A
    testament to a gesture – or a failing.

Fear

The lady who often sang the blues
Came with unexpected views.
'I get up and every day, I'm terrified...
... it's what I am...' And I must say, I find that
Easy to understand. The colossal – all constricting
Fear, that grips the eyes, from ear to ear.

It arrives uninvited and of its own accord.
Always felt but never seen and seldom heard.
Unclog, the cogs of the mind, then with open
Eyes, realize, that it hasn't gone away.
Just circled round the back, of yesterday's moments,
Which allowed you to relax and
Put that unexpected spring, in your every step.

To make an un-welcomed return and leave
A scorch-mark on your ticking mind, to find
Another way to shoulder its every burden.
The days that might skip in other ways, without that weight
Are strictures of time and anxious pauses.
We often long for the lighter touch, where
A little can say or do, much more than the heavy
Sweep of a hand, burdened by its own constraints.

But to ask to wash away the fear
Is to ask to do away with here.
It is much more than a mark on times past.
A reconfiguration of all that's now. A furrow ploughed
Into a future, seeded all with hope. Not
Another bosh shot, doomed to come up short.
Caught betwixt and between, don't fear of being
Seen to fail. Or fear, it's naught to all avail.

Fear can be a pulse of course. A reminder that
The needle on the tank has not yet made the
Empty rank. So if it's got you just a bit, or maybe bites
Ever deeper, take the pinch as news, that you've
Still got something of worth, to give. Fear, can even
Then, be fuel to live.

In Remembrance

Station bound, the other day, I found myself along the way,
Caught out, stone alone, by the War Memorial.
Here striding to the unknown, with sloping rifle,
Helmet and pack, stands the everyman, of national memory.

Around the plinth, lay a swathe of wreathes, made
Melancholy, in the fallen rain and held translucent at
The going down of the sun. The expression chiseled on the
One above, suggested almost fun; which it clearly wasn't.

And what it was – or what it became – becomes less clear
With each diluting, dismembering year.
Orders? Belief? Conviction?… Destiny? Fear? Conscription?
Hard for us now to say. So we imagine. And transpose
Our sentiments – as in a play – convinced he went,
Without a fuss. Just for us.

As with the turning of a page, we age. He does not.
Caught in the moment, along the way, to an ending
That may be either death, or victory – maybe both?
He's a slimmer, younger, braver version, of our older sloth.
We can think the outcome as it may be.
And just as well mate – it was you; and not me.

Some Thoughts on The Execution of Kim Chol, Vice Minister of The North Korean Army, with a Mortar Round

Kim Chol
Was a very naughty boy.
In fact, he was a wrong 'un,
Said Kim Jong-un.

So they stood him on the ground
Where he thought he was safe and sound.
There was even a little song he sang
Before the mortar round went 'bang'.

And as he sailed upwards through the sky
With just a twinkle in his eye
It wasn't the time or place
But perhaps there was a smile upon his face?

For if he thought of the merry dance
In 1797, they led in France.
And many other places before or since
Where they chopped you up for mince.

The guillotine does not recall
For whom it was chosen to fall.
It cares not for hope or luck
But just gets on, with a cold and messy cut.

Poor old Mr. Chol.
It was not an ending filled with joy.
Instead of mourning Kim Jong-il
He ran up a stately bill.

For Scotch and beer and wine.
And it really wasn't the time.
And they were looking for a goat to scape.
To make others contemplate.

The new regime's in town.
So get the hatches battened down.
You thought that black's alright.
But we're telling you now – it's white.

But take it upon my word,
This is all a double edged sword.
If it goes around one day
It comes around they say.

So Kim Jong-un would be wise to know
It's not just pies that make you grow.
Wisdom doesn't always come with age.
And it's seldom found in rage.

And if you're so keen to dish it out
There's really not much doubt.
One day, I'm afraid it's true
There'll be a mortar round for you.

To avoid that unhappy fate
Try to make a date.
And try to realize why
It's about something more than just you and I.

Shattered

'Shattered', came the swift reply, when I, enquiring of the
    moment
Asked away, on a day, much like any other, how things were.
And in these times, when seeing past ourselves is often a task
That becomes too much, even for the best of us, when asked –

It struck me as most appropriate, to be informed, that a feat
Of clay, was now frozen liquid glass. Disregarding of its
Sharded self and whatever else may come to pass.
Un-contemplative of a life of smithereens; of discarded moans
And ups and downs and in-betweens.

And by the assertion of an act of finality, as momentary
As a passing breath, we reassure ourselves of a
Cut glass resurrection, always adding up to something
Short of death. In these days, upon our little stage,
It's unsurprising 'Shattered' is all the rage.

Apologia Pro Vita Sua

Holy Orders aren't my thing and I can't take all that Cardinal
 bling.
But Newman held to his own calling and gave full vent to front
 and
Ground and held his actions to his own conscience sound.
 And nice it
Would be for me to say, on this or every other occasion 'That
 was me!'
On this or any given day.

To build a castle, stone by stone, with each passing year and
 stand
Alone, in the face of whatever tempest life throws your way,
 month
On month and year on year. Moats and drawbridge; keeps and
Battlements held ramrod to the night. Unbending in the fight,
 of
Each day's calling. Strengthening always; never falling.

By twenty-one the plan's laid down, expansion strides across
 the ground.
Thirties come and on we go. A surer triumph is all we know.
And by the time of decade four, we really think we'll always
 score.
But somewhere, after that, there grips a sense of falter.
 Inevitably,
We change and alter. And time that was at our command, calls
 us
Now with its own demands.

One by one, certainties take flight and disappear from view
and
Doubts set in – and doubts renew. And walls made fast by
stone and iron
Crack. And seem to lack the 'forever' that made them an
everlasting redoubt.
The belief of all for one, is spun away. And once a half a
century comes into
Play, the sense of advance, once all pervading, fades from
marble to
A shading. A wish spun on threads of moonlight, made
vapours by the day.

The harder you stand, the more the ground slips away,
beneath you.
Long before the final bend, the route comes harder to defend.
Long before that point is reached, you've learnt there is only
Failure in reach. I'm out of bullets, stones and arrows. Fear
pervades –
The options narrow. One last step. Front foot forward.
I'll fall… but not on my own sword.

A Breeze In The Beeches

Down in the heart of the Wild Wood, unseen,
Things were not all they should have been.
'I say, Badger,' said Toad, 'I see
The Government says you've got T.B.!'

'What the Government says, you can never tell,'
Said Badger, reflectively. 'I'm perfectly well.'
'We should drink to that!' said Moley to Rat.
'You can never tell. That's definitely a fact.'

'But this talk of gas, it's not very nice.
It's spooked all the weasels and frightened the mice.'
Toad stroked his waistcoat. 'You know what I say?
I think it's time for a long holiday.'

'We'll pack up the cases and load up the car.
Take the open road and travel as far
As the inclination takes us, we've plenty of time.
Get to the seaside. I'm sure it'll be fine.'

All were as one and they collectively agreed
To take in the country and a bit of sea breeze.
So they grabbed their cases and packed what they could.
It was 'Goodbye!' for now to their beloved Wild Wood.

But outside the door, they were met with a surprise
A forest of gun barrels assailed their eyes.
It seemed unlikely they would get very far.
In fact it was certain, they wouldn't make the car.

They were massacred together, side by side.
Very similar in fact, to Bonnie and Clyde.
Rat raised his paws. 'I surrender to you!'
But they took no notice and blew him in two.

Toad tried running, it was far too late.
They cut him to pieces at a quarter to eight.
When the firing was over, all that was left of Mole
Was the frayed circumference of a very large hole.

Badger's corpse was riddled with lead.
And they kept on firing, long after he was dead.
When the shooting was over and the smoke had cleared
There was plenty of reason to give a good cheer.

It was just as intended; they planned it this way.
And the news was broken on 'Farming Today'.
Defra was resplendent in flexing its muscles.
And two hours later they were cheering in Brussels.

They doubled their expenses to satisfy their hunger
And called up Silvio and ordered some 'Bunga'.
The moral of this story, as I'm sure you can tell –
'They Govern for You!' And they govern jolly well.

For Nick Drake

Your voice is clearer now in starlight, than it ever was, in the
Twilight of your lifetime. Ten thousand nights have come
And gone, on a journey day long, long ago surrendered but
Remembered still, down the days of Fall and all, the
    recollected
Laze of broken early mornings. Songs of unforgotten callings,
Cluster chords that still fulfil and more – the purpose you
    intended.

And I still lament, with full intent, all the lakes of tranquil
    glaze,
Fed by icy falls of wonder, that we never got to hear,
When that evening passed unclear and you slipped beyond
This world's grasp, towards another calling.
But all remains are framed within the span of works began,
    with
Lyric lines and the acoustic chimes, that spoke of journeys
    earned
And lent, that sometimes sent us, more than we could, at first,
    ever reason.

And did you tell the man, about the plan, for Lilac Time?
And would the sky have cleared and would you have cheered
For Betty's smile? All you sang and wrote, note on note
Was not just for you but all of us, if only more had stopped
To listen. And alone upon a stage of your own mind, there
Are none to see beyond your beaming leaps of wounded
    aspirations.

Keep it spare; lean to the bone of what it is that really matters.
Find a truth, though small but with all the prospects of a
    brighter future.
You may be gone, long gone but in every word, in every song,
    counts the
Moment down for us, in all our every different stages. The
    spirals of this
World, aged you out of it, far too soon. And under a different
    sun or another
Moon, we might know – How they Come and Go. How they
    Come and Go.

Hello!

The other day, the splendid Duke of Cambridge, came to say
'Hello! Nice to meet you. Just the life! And I've brought
Along my charming wife.' New hairstyles, coats and shoes.
'We'd love to hear your latest news.'

Crowds and crowds to meet and greet and view majestically
In one fell sweep. They line six deep in the Market Square
And stop and gawp and click and cheer. For all our laments
     and current
Regret, we may be frayed bananas but no republic – yet.

Live Free or Die

'Live Free or Die!' should be proclaimed, of course, by a man,
Rifle in hand, boots and chaps and ten gallon hat, astride a
    horse.
Instead, it's the motto of the Granite State and generally seen
    on the
Number plates of passing cars. Makes me wonder, if they do?

Here on narrow pavements, once made for two, teem the faces
    lined with
Blank dismay, long before any rainbow's end comes into view.
People drifting, as less than they otherwise would. Vexed by
    more
Than just the moment. Long before this month's pay day
    comes – it's spent,
For ill – or good.

Faces fat and gaunt. Starved of belief – hollowed out, by each
    day's dose of
Disappointment. On the tow path, bathed in the long shadows
    of winter light,
Comes the man, can warming in his hand, urging on his
    canine friend,
Who sleek with curiosity, checks the ground, with sober strides –
He seeks a place for man and dog to hide.

The one who rides tall in the saddle, still has countless miles
    left to travel.
For us, perception's scars are always just a step too far.
Imperceptibly, we wind down and give it all away to luck.
'Live Free or Die!' is not a concept these days, on the up.

Another Year's Going

Comes the frost that's hard to crack, the creeping freeze of
    fog, that makes it half
Missed looking back. Memory leaps and fails, down the creeps
    and pools and
Moments of short inhales, that makes the bricks and mortar of
    what was, or
Ought to be, another year gone by. Try as we otherwise may, it
    always leaves us
Standing, caught short by fallen fact, half hoping something
    better's coming up
The unseen track.

These dozen months or more, or half, or twice the score, of all
    we sort or
Aimed for. They stretch back, like unlettered milestones along
    the straights and
Bends, of where we've been and the ones to come as yet
    unseen, from where
We find ourselves, still standing. And what a decade back
    seemed too far ahead
To think, is now consigned to pangs of wasted time. The small
    pawn of regret, takes
Quietly, every knight of trepidation we've ever met.

Index of first lines